Picturesque Word Origins

PICTURESQUE WORD ORIGINS

With forty-five Illustrative Drawings

REG. U.S.PAT.OFF.

G. & C. Merriam Company, Springfield, Massachusetts, U. S. A.

This facsimile edition produced in 2011 by Merriam-Webster, Incorporated
and printed by HGI Company.

ISBN 978-0-87779-597-1

MADE IN U.S.A.

SET UP AND ELECTROTYPED BY D. B. UPDIKE, THE MERRYMOUNT PRESS

BOSTON, MASS.

PRINTED AND BOUND BY H. O. HOUGHTON & CO., THE RIVERSIDE PRESS

CAMBRIDGE, MASS.

Publisher's Preface

PICTURESQUE WORD ORIGINS is an exotic amongst the many books published by Merriam-Webster. A slender volume with an unusual page size, featuring large type, generous margins, and well-spaced lines, it stands in contrast to other Merriam-Webster books, noted for their utilitarian design and many pages of densely set type. Freed from the need to fit as much text as possible on every page, the design of this book has but one goal: to please the eye with every aspect of the page. The result is a book that is startling in its simplicity, its elegance, and its charm.

Picturesque Word Origins was published in 1933, and the company (then the G. & C. Merriam Co.) clearly intended it to be a very special book. To create it, they turned to Daniel Berkeley Updike, a book designer whose books were known for their clarity of organization and easy readability. His Merrymount Press in Boston, where he worked in collaboration with John Bianchi, created some of the most beautifully designed and printed books of the era, including *The Book of Common Prayer* and Izaak Walton's *The Compleat Angler*.

For the text of the entries, Updike chose Janson, a sturdy Old Style typeface that he was increasingly relying upon in the 1930s, most notably in *The Book of Common Prayer*. The headwords are hand-set in Garamond bold, printed in red, and are one of the most pleasing aspects of the book. Updike seldom used Garamond, but for this book, a boldface type was appropriate, and Garamond's subtle boldface was ideal.

The illustrations are zinc etchings from line drawings by Louis Szanto, a Hungarian-born painter and etcher. He came to this country in the early 1930s and worked on projects commissioned by the Works Progress Administration, and his murals, depicting stories from history and literature, still hang in public spaces.

Recognition for the success of this effort came quickly, as the book was named one of the Fifty Books of the Year by the American Institute of Graphic Arts in 1934.

For this new printing, we have preserved the text as written in 1933. We considered reediting the text to remove insensitive language, but to do so would have required resetting lines and marring the appearance of the original pages. We hope readers will appreciate that the book is a product of its time and not let the differing sensibilities of that era spoil their enjoyment of this otherwise delightful book.

Readers should also keep in mind that the scholarship behind the stories told here is that of the then-current *Webster's New International Dictionary*, published in 1909. Much has been learned about the etymology of words since then, and today's readers should also consult a more recently published dictionary.

The original goals of the *Picturesque Word Origins* are clear — to delight readers and foster an interest in the history of words. Merriam-Webster is pleased to reissue this book in the confidence that it will delight and fascinate readers once again.

Introduction

BACK of almost every word in the English language there is a "life story" that will come to the average reader as a fascinating revelation. Our words have come to us from sources and in ways that will prove most surprising to anyone who has not before discovered the delights of tracing words back to their origins. Some of them have lived for thousands of years and have played their parts in many lands and many civilizations. They may record ancient superstitions. They may be monuments to customs dating back to classical antiquity. They may reveal the manners and beliefs of ancestors shrouded in the mists of ancient history. Words that you use to-day may have been the slang of Roman soldiers twenty centuries ago or the lingo of a Malay savage. They may have been used by an Athenian poet or by an Anglo-Saxon farmer. Thousands of our words are, in themselves, miniatures from the history of humanity—glimpses of episodes in the growth of civilization, pictures of life in a dim past.

This little book offers merely a taste of the wonders of word origins. Its purpose is to demonstrate the extraordinary interest of a subject that has always hidden behind the forbidding name *etymology*.

The information presented in this book is taken from WEBSTER'S NEW INTERNATIONAL DICTIONARY, which is famous for the completeness and scholarliness of its etymologies. The word stories which follow are but a few chosen at random. Many thousands more may be found in WEBSTER'S NEW INTERNATIONAL DICTIONARY, to which readers who wish to pursue this fascinating study are referred.

Picturesque Word Origins

Abet

PICTURESQUE WORD ORIGINS

Abet: *from the baiting of wild animals*

From the ancient sport of bear baiting, the English language has taken a violent word and applied it to men rather than to animals. *Abet* goes far back to an old Teutonic origin that conjures up a picture of hardy men going to the chase with their packs of hunting dogs. Our English verb *bite* appeared long ago in a Low German derivative *bētan*, meaning "to cause to bite," "to make bite," as, to *make* dogs *bite* the bear, and so to *send* them *out to hunt* the bear. Icelandic *beita* meant "to feed," "make bite," and also "to hunt" with dogs. The French adopted both the sport and the Teutonic name for it, making the Old French verb *beter*, meaning "to bait" a bear, and *abeter*, "to excite," "incite," which we have taken into English as *abet*. No longer applied to the hunt, it now means to encourage or incite persons, usually in an evil enterprise.

Abeyance: *waiting with gaping mouth*

Something "held in abeyance" may cause some anxiety or impatience, but it hardly suggests "open-mouthed expectancy." Yet that was originally the literal meaning of the word *abeyance*. It comes from the Late Latin *badare*, "to gape." The word passed into the Old French form *baer*, *beer*, "to gape," "to look with open mouth," "to expect." From this was derived the Old French *abeance*, literally, "a gaping at," but used metaphorically to express "expectation" or "longing." This is the English *abeyance*, a legal term used of rights which were suspended, "held in abeyance," awaiting a proper claimant. Its meaning, however, has broadened in general use to denote any kind of suspension or temporary suppression.

Abject: *literally, thrown away*

A transition from the literal to the figurative, and from cause to effect, has occurred in the meaning of *abject*. *Ab*, meaning "off," "away," and *jacere*, meaning "to throw," were combined in Latin to form *abjicere*, "to throw away," with a past participle *abjectus*, "thrown away." Directly from this source came the English word *abject*, which was formerly not only an adjective but also a verb meaning "to cast off," "to throw down," and, with a figurative application, "to degrade." It is this latter meaning that survives in the Modern English adjective *abject* which characterizes one who has been cast off or degraded and who is therefore low in condition or cast down in spirit.

Abominate: *to shrink from an evil omen*

To the ancient Romans an *omen* was a sign from the gods—a promise of good or a warning of evil. Naturally, they turned away in fear from an evil omen. To express this aversion they combined *ab*, "away," and *omen*, "a foreboding," into the verb *abominari*, meaning "to deprecate as ominous," "to abhor," with a past participle *abominatus*, the source of English *abominate*. The word has largely lost its original connotation of dread and has come to mean "to loathe," "to despise."

Abrupt: *broken off*

Rumpere, in Latin, means "to break," "to burst." With the prefix *ab*, "off," Latin formed *abrumpere*, "to break off." The past participle *abruptus* gives the English word *abrupt*, "broken off." In Modern

English this meaning has been applied figuratively to the manner of a person who speaks or acts suddenly and curtly, or to things that change suddenly—"breaking off" unexpectedly.

Rupture is an English word that still retains the literal meaning of "bursting," as do *disrupt* and *interrupt*, all derived from the same *rumpere. Corrupt*, however, is figurative: "broken faith."

Abundance: *in a wave*

Nothing suggests great abundance more vividly than overflowing waves—and that is the literal meaning of the word *abundance*. In Latin, *unda* means "wave," poetically "sea." The Romans combined *ab*, "from," and *unda* into the word *abundare*, "to overflow"—literally, "to come from the waves" or "from the sea"—applied to anything very plentiful. The stem of *abundare* gave the English verb *abound*, and a derivative gave the noun *abundance*.

Inundate, "to flood," also comes from *unda*, as does *undulate*, "to move like the waves."

Accost: *rib to rib*

Costa is the Latin word for "rib," and hence "side." With the prefix *ad*, "to," it formed the Latin verb *accostare* meaning "to bring to the side of," "to bring side by side." From this or from the French derivative *accoster*, we have made English *accost*, which first meant "to lie alongside," then "to come alongside," "to approach," "to approach and greet," and finally simply "to greet," "to speak to."

Accumulate: *to pile up*

When, in colloquial speech, a man refers to the accumulating of a fortune as "making his pile," he is using exactly the same figurative language as that which first suggested the word *accumulate*. *Cumulus* is Latin for "a heap or pile," and *cumulare* means "to pile up." With the prefix *ad*, "to," we have *accumulare*, "to heap together," which is the source of our English word *accumulate*.

Accurate: *done with care*

To do a thing accurately, one must do it carefully—as even the etymology of the word suggests. Latin *cura* means "care," and *accurare* means "to expend care on," "to take care of." The past participle *accuratus* means "done with care," and from it we have made our word *accurate*.

Achieve: *to bring things to a head*

To achieve something is to bring plans and action to a head. This is the literal meaning of the ancestor of our word *achieve*, which was borrowed from the French in Norman times. They had made the verb *achever* out of the preposition *a*, "to," and *chief*, "head": "to bring to a head." Old French *chief* comes, in turn, through a thousand years of gradual changes, which only the strongest (accented) syllables survived, from Latin *caput*, "head." The original sense, "bring to a head," easily acquired the present significance, "bring to a successful conclusion," "make a success" of the task in hand.

Acumen: *the sharpness of the mind*

A keen mind may be likened to a sharp knife, which penetrates easily and quickly. For clean-cut action, both the knife and the mind must be sharp. So it is natural that, when a word was needed to denote the faculty of keen, penetrating thought, the Latin word for "sharpness" should be borrowed. *Acuere*, in Latin, means "to sharpen," and *acumen* means "sharpness." English borrowed *acumen* and used it figuratively for sharpness of the mind.

Acumen

Acute, from the past participle of the same Latin verb *acuere*, means "sharpened," "keen," and is used broadly in a figurative sense.

Affluent: *with flowing riches*

The metaphor of the tides that we find in the word *abundance* is found also in *affluent*. Latin *affluere* means "to flow to," from *ad*, "to," and *fluere*, "to flow." From its present participle, English borrowed *affluent*, originally in the literal meaning "to flow toward." Its meaning broadened to "flow freely or abundantly." Then a figurative use developed, "flowing with riches," "wealthy."

Aftermath: *the second mowing*

Math is Old English for "a mowing" or the "crop" gathered by mowing. *Math* is a noun made from the old root of the verb *mow* (*māwan* in Old English) with the suffix *-th* which we find in *grow-th*, "a growing," from the verb *grow*, and *bir-th* from the verb *bear*, "give birth to." *After-math* is the "after-mowing" or "second mowing," that is, the crop of grass that grew up and was cut after the first had been harvested. This was an appropriate figure of speech for after-effects or consequences in general; so we may now say "the *aftermath* of a battle."

Aggravate: *to make heavy*

The Latin word *gravis* means "heavy," and *aggravare* means "to make heavy." From the past participle *aggravatus* English borrowed *aggravate*, "to make heavy, weighty, serious, grievous." Then the sense becomes transferred from the *thing* which is made grievous to the person who is annoyed by it, and *aggravate* acquires the sense of "provoke," "annoy," sometimes thoughtlessly used in a flippant sense, as, an "*aggravating* shoestring."

Agony: *from an ancient athletic meet*

It is strange that a word which denotes anguish and intolerable pain should have its origin in a festive sport event; yet that is the case with *agony*. In ancient Greece, *agōn* was a public assembly, especially one for public games and athletic contests. *Agonia* was the contest or struggle for the prize. From the meaning "a struggle for victory in the games," *agonia* gradually broadened to mean any physical struggle, an activity fraught with difficulty or pain, and then mental anguish as well. Our own word *agony*, borrowed from this source, meant struggle or anguish of mind, then the throes of death, and hence any extreme suffering of body or mind.

Agony

L. SZANTO

Alarm: *a call to arms*

From the old French summons to battle *a l'arme!* "to arms!" it seems a far cry to the modern alarm clock; yet that is actually the scope of the word's development. *A l'arme!* was first the call itself and then, in the form *alarme*, it became the name of this sudden summons. The English *alarm*, which comes from this origin, first had the same meaning, but gradually broadened to denote a warning signal of any kind of danger, and then the apparatus for giving this signal, such as a fire bell. Perhaps the clock which rings in the morning is suggestive of a fire bell, or perhaps it rings a warning that it is time to get up—however that may be, it is called an *alarm* clock.

It is interesting to note also that *alarm* has developed an additional meaning—the fear which results from a warning of danger.

Alert: *to the lookout point!*

Alert had its origin in a military phrase of an earlier day and another land. The first step back takes us to the French *alerte*, really a phrase: *à l'erte*, meaning "on the watch." This in turn was borrowed from Italian *all' erta*, "on the watch," properly, standing "on the height" where one can look around, from *erta*, a "declivity" or "steep," literally, a place "raised up," from Latin *erectus*, "erected." Our English word *alert* first carried the original meaning of "vigilant" but has broadened to denote also "quick in action," and "lively in manner."

Alimony: *feeding the estranged wife*

Alimony can be called literally a "meal ticket" when we consider the original source of the word. It is borrowed from the Latin *alimonia*, "nourishment," "sustenance," from *alere*, "to nourish." The primitive English meaning was "maintenance" or "the means of livelihood," a meaning which is now overshadowed by the use of the word in connection with separated couples.

Alphabet: *a and b*

Just as we refer to our A B C's, using the first three letters to mean the complete list, as a whole, so the Greeks used *alpha* and *beta*, their names for "a" and "b," the first two letters. The combination of these two, *alpha + beta*, is the origin of the English word *alphabet*.

Ambiguous: *wandering about*

Latin *amb-*, "about," "around," combined with *agere*, "to drive," formed *ambigere*, literally, "to drive about," "to wander about," "to waver." Out of this word grew the Latin *ambiguus*, "hesitating," "uncertain." English borrowed it as *ambiguous*, with the meaning "equivocal," "capable of being understood in either of two or more possible senses," "vague."

Ambition: *a going about for votes*

Even in ancient Rome candidates for public office went about soliciting votes. This activity was denoted by the word *ambitio*, "a going about, around." *Ambitio* was derived from *ambire*, "to go about," which in turn was formed from *amb-*, "about," and *ire*, "to go." Since this activity indicated a desire for honor or power, the word *ambitio* came to mean the desire for official honors. This word was borrowed in French and English as *ambition*, and its meaning broadened to denote the earnest desire for preferment or achievement.

Ambulance: *a walking hospital*

When the needs of war first brought into use the temporary field hospital, organized to follow

Ambition

an army, the French gave it the quaint name *hôpital ambulant*, "walking hospital," from the Latin *ambulare*, "to walk." Eventually *hôpital* was dropped and the adjective *ambulant* was replaced by the noun *ambulance*. The meaning has changed slightly from "moving hospital" to a vehicle for transporting injured or sick persons to a hospital.

Anatomy: *cutting up the body*

Our knowledge of human *anatomy*, that is, the structure of the body, was acquired through experimental dissection, and the word *anatomy* itself records this method of acquiring the knowledge. The Greek word for dissection, and the ancestor of our word *anatomy*, is *anatomē*, formed from *ana*, "up," and a root which appears in the verb *temnein*, "to cut." The primary meaning of *anatomy* is the "cutting up" or dissecting of a body to learn its structure, and from this come the now commoner meanings, "science of the structure of a body" and the "structure" itself.

Anecdote: *unpublished notes*

Even among the ancient Greeks there were two kinds of stories—those given out publicly and those known only privately. The latter kind was called *anekdotos*, "not published." The word was

Anecdote

formed by combining *a, an,* "not," and *ekdotos,* "given out." From this source comes French *anecdote* and thence English *anecdote,* which originally retained the Greek significance of "unpublished narratives." But an "unpublished narrative," especially about interesting things and famous people, has a ready market; so *anecdotes* are eagerly brought out on every occasion, and the word loses its original sense, coming to mean simply "a story," "an incident."

Anniversary: *the turn of a year*

The year rolls around to bring the *anniversary* of birth, marriage, or some other event—and this "turning" of the year is the literal meaning of the word *anniversary.* The word is borrowed from Latin *anniversarius,* from *annus,* "year," and *vertere* (past participle, *versus*), "to turn."

Anthem: *originally, responsive singing*

The word *anthem* has lost its etymological meaning. It now means simply "a hymn" but it was formerly a composition sung responsively, that is, with parts sung by two alternating voices or choruses. This original meaning is indicated in the original word, which was Greek *antiphōna,* from *anti,* "over against," and *phōnē,* "sound," "voice." *Antiphōna,* through the Latin (of the early

Arrive

Christian missionaries), comes into Anglo-Saxon as *antefen*, Middle English *antefne* and *antym*, Modern English *anthem*.

Arrive: *to come to shore*

Latin *ad* means "to" and *ripa* means "shore" or "sloping bank of a river." These two words combined are found in Late Latin *arripare*, "to come to shore." Old French in the course of centuries changed the word into the form *ariver*, and Medieval (Middle) English borrowed it as *ariven*, meaning "to land." The meaning broadened from "going ashore" to mean reaching a point in any way. To-day, when we *arrive* by automobile or airplane, it is interesting to think of the original meaning, "to come to shore."

Assassin: *a drinker of hashish*

In eleventh-century Persia, a secret order was founded among the Ismaili, a Mohammedan sect, by Hassan ben Sabbah. The absolute head of this order was the Old Man of the Mountain. Its members indulged in the use of the Oriental drug hashish, and, when under its influence, in the fanatical practice of secret murder. This terrible organization spread terror over Persia, Syria, and

Assassin

LOUIS SZANTO

Asia Minor for nearly two centuries. The murderous drinker of hashish came to be called *hash-shāsh*, "one who has drunk of the hashish," and from that origin comes our English word *assassin*.

Astonish: *actually, thunderstruck*

When we trace our Modern English word *astonish* back through the Middle English *astonien* and Old French *estoner*, we find its original source in Latin *ex*, "out," combined with *tonare*, "to thunder." The first meaning of *astonish* was "to stun," "to render senseless," as by a thunderbolt or a blow. But the word has lost its physical significance and now suggests great surprise, sudden fear, or wonder.

Athlete: *one who contends for a prize*

The ancestor of our modern *athlete* was the ancient Greek or Roman who entered the public games as a prize fighter or a contestant for a prize. The word *athlete* is borrowed from Latin *athleta* and that, in turn, from Greek *athlētēs*, "prize fighter." This word was formed from *athlein*, "to contend for a prize," from *athlos*, "a contest," and *athlon*, "a prize."

Astonish

Auction: *increasing the price*

"I'm offered five dollars! Will anyone make it six? Who'll make it six dollars for this beautiful vase? Six dollars, thank you! I'm offered six dollars! Who'll make it six-fifty?" Anyone who has attended an *auction* knows how the auctioneer develops the bidding into an "increasing" price. And there we find the literal meaning of the word. *Auction* comes from Latin *auctio*, "an increasing," from the verb *augere*, "to increase."

Auspicious: *a favorable flight of birds*

In ancient Rome the flight of birds was studied for omens, good or bad, that would forecast the success or failure of an enterprise. From *avis*, "bird," and the root of *specere*, "to see," was formed the word *auspex*, meaning "a bird seer"—one who observed the flight of birds and read the portent of them. *Auspicium* meant "divination." From this comes the word *auspicious* which means "full of omen," but especially "full of good omen," "giving promise of success."

Ballot: *once a little ball*

Before the days of printed forms and voting machines, secret voting was done (as it still is in many clubs) with little balls. From the Italian *balla*, "ball," and its diminutive *ballotta*, "little ball," English borrowed *ballot*, "a little ball used for secret voting," which remains to designate the printed slip we now use in voting. We even "cast our ballot" by pulling a lever. And, by extension, the word signifies the act of voting and the privilege of voting as well as the whole number of votes cast at an election.

Bank: *originally, the table of a money changer*

The etymology of our word *bank* carries us back to the infancy of financial operations. We borrowed the word from French *banque*, which, in turn, was borrowed from Italian *banca*, originally "bench," "table," or "counter," the table or counter of a money changer. *Bank* came to be applied to the money changer's place of business; its meaning broadened with the development of banking, and it now means the building or office used for banking purposes, or the institution and its representatives.

Bedlam: *really, a madhouse*

In 1247 the priory of St. Mary of Bethlehem was founded in London. In the early fifteenth cen-

Bedlam

tury it came to be used as a hospital for lunatics. Familiarly known as *Bethlehem*, the name of this asylum was contracted in popular usage to *Bethlem*, *Bedlem*, or *Bedlam*. The name came to be applied to any lunatic asylum, and consequently, in our own day, *bedlam* is used to signify any scene of uproar or confusion that is suggestive of a madhouse.

Belfry: *the war tower of medieval England*

Strangely enough, the origin of our word *belfry* has nothing to do with bells. It is even more surprising that this word, which now suggests peace and good will, once denoted an instrument of war. In medieval Germany, two words, *bergen*, "to protect," and *vride*, "peace," "security," were combined to form *bercvrit*, the name of a movable war tower used by besiegers. A form of this word was borrowed in Old French as *berfrei*, and thence into Middle English as *berfray*, with the same meaning. It was only a step from the meaning "siege tower" to the meaning "watch-tower," and then to any tower. The custom of putting bells in towers made people think that *berfray* ought really to be *bell-fray*, and gradually both the pronunciation and the meaning of the word were changed by this ignorant usage, an example of what is known as "popular etymology." In Modern English, *belfry* means exclusively a "bell tower," or the bell room atop a tower.

Belfry

L. SZANTO

Bible: *from the papyrus of the ancient Egyptians*

The world's earliest form of paper was made by the Egyptians from the papyrus, a reed native to the Nile Valley. The pith of this plant was sliced and pressed into a sheet which was used for writing. The Greek word for this material was *biblos*. The first books were long, rolled-up sheets of papyrus, and so *biblos* came to mean "a volume," "a book." It was borrowed into Latin as a plural, *biblia*, whence are derived French *bible* and English *bible*. The word in English (Chaucer) originally might mean simply "a book" but was used to designate the Scriptures and eventually became *The Book* or *The Bible*.

Paper takes its name from the papyrus plant, Greek *papyros*, Latin *papyrus*, French *papier*, whence English *paper*.

Book is of Teutonic origin. The ancient Saxons and Germans used pieces of beech on which to write by scratching (the original sense of Anglo-Saxon *wrītan*, "write"). The Anglo-Saxon word for "beech" was *bōc*, which came to designate the writing on beech boards, the "book." Medieval English called it *bok* and *book*.

Still another word of similar origin is *code*, which comes from the Latin *codex*, meaning the stock or stem of a tree and hence boards or tablets of wood smeared over with wax which served the ancients as writing tablets.

Bless: *a reminder of the ancient consecration by blood*

Bless is one of those interesting words whose history carries us back to the old Anglo-Saxon days and suggests the customs of that ancient race. *Bless* comes to us directly from the Middle English *blessien*, which, in turn, was derived from Anglo-Saxon *blētsian*. *Blētsian* came from the Anglo-Saxon *blōd* meaning "blood," and its original meaning probably was "to consecrate by blood." Although through the centuries the word has lost its association with the thought of blood, our modern *bless* is etymologically a reminder of the living sacrifices of ancient days.

Bombastic: *speech stuffed with cotton*

In Late Latin *bombax* means "cotton." Through the Old French form *bombace*, the word came into English as *bombast*. Its original meaning in English was "cotton"; then it broadened to mean any soft fibrous material used as stuffing for garments, and in time took on the general meaning

Bonfire

"stuffing" or "padding." These meanings are all obsolete but the word *bombast* lives on, for it was applied metaphorically to "inflated style"—speech that is "stuffed" and "padded" with high-sounding words.

Bonfire: *a fire of bones*

In the Middle Ages, funeral pyres for human bodies were a necessity in emergencies of war or pestilence. *Bonefires* (fires of bone) they were called. Later, when the custom of burning heretics at the stake became common, *bonefires* was the name applied to the pyres of these victims. The same term was used to designate the burning of symbols of heresy or other proscribed articles. Later, its meaning was extended to open-air fires for public celebrations or sports—but by this time in the less gruesome spelling *bonfire*, which to-day is a comparatively harmless word despite its grim history.

Bribe: *once only a scrap of bread*

The word *bribe* has degenerated morally while acquiring greater importance financially. It was once an honest scrap of bread. That was in the Late Latin form *briba*. The French borrowed it (*bribe*)

Bribe

in the sense "a lump of bread," "leavings of meals," something that might be given to beggars. When *bribe* first came into English it meant "a gift begged," then "a present." In modern use the "present" is frequently a large amount of money, and its purpose is to corrupt a person in a position of trust.

Broker: *originally, a retail vendor of wine*

The modern *broker* who engages in large-scale financial operations takes his name from a humble origin. *Broker* (spelled in Middle English *brocour*) appears to be derived from Old French *broquier* or *brokier*, dialect for *brochier*, "a broacher," "one who broaches or taps" a cask to draw off the liquor. The modern verb *broach*, besides meaning "to tap" a cask, is used in a figurative sense of "to open," as in "the subject was *broached*." So the original *broker* was a retail vendor of wine, and later, any small retailer, middleman, peddler, or agent in general, as a pawn*broker*. More dignified commodities, such as stocks and bonds, have in modern times dignified the *broker* and his occupation.

Budget: *from a little leather bag*

In this age when nations, corporations, and families all have their *budgets*, it is interesting to trace

Broker

the word back to its origin. The Romans had a word, *bulga*, which the Old French borrowed as *bouge*, *boge*, meaning "leather bag." The diminutive form was *bougette*, "bag," "wallet." From this source, through the Middle English form *bogett*, *bouget*, is derived our own word *budget*. The earliest meaning of *budget* was "a pouch or wallet, especially of leather," which suggests, along with its other possible uses, a moneybag or purse. This meaning has become obsolete and *budget* has adapted itself to the more important affairs of modern finance.

Bugle: *from the ox that first supplied it*

The first meaning of *bugle* in Modern English was "a wild ox, especially a buffalo." We can trace the word back to the Middle English *bugle*, "buffalo," then to the French *bugle* which was derived from Latin *buculus*, "a young bullock."

The horn of an ox, made into a blowing instrument, was called a *bugle horn* after the animal which supplied the horn; then *horn* was dropped and *bugle* alone came to be used with the same meaning; and that meaning has been retained while the original meaning "ox" has long been obsolete.

Butcher: *a slaughterer of goats*

Modern diets have given the *butcher* a much more varied function than that which originally was his. What the *butcher* was originally we can find by tracing the word back to its source. *Butcher* comes from Middle English *bocher*, *bochier*, which was borrowed from Old French *bochier*. The Old French *bochier* is a derivative of Old French *boc*, "a buck goat." The original meaning of *bochier* was therefore "a slaughterer of buck goats."

Calculate: *from the counting stones of the Romans*

The Romans had no adding machines. Even the art of writing was known to comparatively few persons. So they did their adding and subtracting with the aid of little stones used as counters. The Latin word for the little stone used in this way was *calculus*, diminutive of *calx* meaning "limestone." From *calculus* the verb *calculare*, "to calculate," was formed, and its past participle, *calculatus*, is the immediate origin of English *calculate*.

Calm: *companion of heat*

"Burning" is more likely to suggest violence than calm, and yet our word *calm* seems to be

Calculate

derived from the Greek word meaning "to burn." Greek *kauma*, "burning heat," a derivative of the root of Greek *kaiein*, "to burn," is borrowed in Late Latin *cauma*, "heat." This seems to be the ancestor of Italian *calma*, French *calme*, and English *calm*. *Calm* has acquired its modern meaning either because during a great heat there is generally also a calm or because the hot time of the day obliges us to seek shade and quiet.

It is interesting to note that from the same Greek root comes our word *caustic* with a meaning thoroughly different from that of *calm*.

Cancel: *from the crossbars of a latticed gate*

The Latin word *cancer* means "lattice." Its diminutive plural form *cancelli* was the origin of *cancellare*, "to make a lattice" of cross lines to obliterate a writing. Our word *cancel* comes from this origin and its meaning has broadened from "the making of cross lines to obliterate writing," to "making void" or revoking in any way.

Candidate: *originally, one clothed in white*

In Latin *candidus* means "glittering," "white." In ancient Rome, a man campaigning for office

Candidate

wore a white toga and was consequently called *candidatus*, "clothed in white." From this comes our word *candidate* with the meaning "one campaigning for office"—but without the original significance as to dress.

From the same Latin word *candidus* we have our adjective *candid*. This word was first used in English with its literal meaning "white" but is now applied figuratively to a mental quality unclouded by dissimulation or bias.

Canopy: *a protection from gnats*

Canopy, which now designates, in general, any overhanging shelter, has strayed far from its literal meaning. It can be traced back to Greek *kōnōps*, "gnat." A derivative *cōnōpeion*, "a bed with mosquito curtains," came into Late Latin as *conopeum*. Old French borrowed *conopeum* as *conopée*, "canopy," "pavilion," and English, in turn, borrowed the French word as *canopy*, which has come to mean not only a covering fixed over a bed but any overhanging shade or shelter.

Carol: *originally, a dance*

Carol is a word which has wandered far from its original meaning. When we search for its origin

Carol

we find it in the Greek *choros*, meaning "dance." This word was combined with *aulein*, "to play on the flute," and formed *choraulēs*, "a flute player who accompanied the choral dance." Through the Latin *choraules* the word developed into the Old French *caroler*, "to dance," and *carole*, "a dance accompanied by singing." In the English form *carol* the word kept its meaning "a round or ring dance accompanied with song." Gradually, however, the meaning of "dance" was lost and "song" alone survived, so that now a *carol* is a song of praise or a ballad of religious joy, as an Easter or Christmas *carol*.

Chapel: *from the sacred cloak of St. Martin*

Late Latin *cappa* meant "cloak," and a diminutive form *cappella*, spelled also *capella*, meant "a little cloak," "a hood," "a cowl." The cloak worn by St. Martin of Tours, who died in the fourth century, was preserved as a holy relic, and the word *capella* was used to refer to the shrine in which St. Martin's cloak was kept. So *capella* came to mean a place for keeping sacred things, and finally any holy place, or place of worship, the meaning of the Old French form *chapele*, taken into English as *chapel*. The guardian of the shrine where St. Martin's cloak was kept was called in Latin *capellanus* which gave French *chapelain*, English *chaplain*.

Chapel

Chivalry: *the quality of knightliness*

Those knights of the Golden Age, with their traditional honor, protective kindness to the weak, and generosity to foes, are immortalized in our word *chivalry*. The knight was a horseman, a rider, in days when the possession of a riding horse was something of a distinction. A knight, a mounted warrior, was called in Old French (also Modern French) *chevalier*, a derivative of *caballus*, "a horse," which, in Vulgar Latin, had replaced the classical Latin *equus*. The characteristic qualities of knighthood, the things a mounted warrior should be, were embraced in the French word *chevalerie*, taken into English as *chivalry*, including bravery, gallantry, and all those endowments of mind and heart suggested by the expression *noblesse oblige*.

Climate: *embodying the Greek idea of the earth's formation*

The ancient Greeks believed that the earth sloped (*klinein* is the Greek verb "to slope") from the equator to the north pole and that this incline accounted for the varied climates of the different zones. So, to designate a region or zone of the earth the Greeks used the word *klima*, with a stem *klimat-*, formed from the verb *klinein*, "to slope." The word was borrowed by Latin as *clima, cli-*

matis, and from Latin it was taken into French as *climat*, and into English as *climate*, now used to denote the general state of weather in a region.

Coin: *from the instrument that first made it*

Our word *coin* is derived from the Latin *cuneus* meaning "wedge," and then "die for stamping money." The French form of the word is *coin*, taken into English first in the old sense of "die for stamping money," then coming to mean the "impression of the die," or the "piece of metal stamped with the die."

Companion: *one who shares bread with another*

"Breaking bread" together is an ancient rite of friendship. And it is the literal meaning of *companion*, for this word is derived from Late Latin *companio*, with a stem *companion-*, which was formed from *com-*, "with," and *panis*, "bread." One who shares bread with another is naturally in his company for a longer or shorter period, and consequently the word *companion* has taken on the meaning "one who accompanies another," with no longer any particular reference to sharing bread.

Comrade, while its modern meaning is similar to *companion*, comes to us from a different source.

It is derived from Latin *camera* (*camara*) "a chamber." A *comrade* was, then, "one who shares a room"; *comrades* lived in the same dwelling. But the meaning of the word has broadened, and *comrades* now may be those who merely work or play together.

Complexion: *a revelation of disposition*

Latin *complexio* means "a braiding or weaving together" (*com-*, "with," and *plectere*, "to braid, weave"). It was used in the Middle Ages to mean the combination of the four qualities: hot, cold, moist, dry, whose proportions were supposed to determine the nature of anything. Thus, the *complexion* of water was said to be cold and moist; that of fire was said to be hot and dry. *Complexion* was also used to denote the combination of the four humors or fluids supposed by medieval physiologists to exist in the body in varying proportions which determined the character of a person: blood, phlegm, choler (yellow bile), melancholy (black bile). Thus, a man was said to be of a sanguine (red-blooded) or of a melancholy *complexion* or character. Since the color of the skin generally indicates something of the nature or character of a person, the word *complexion* came to be applied to the outward signs, especially to the color of the face.

Compunction: *pricking of the conscience*

When we speak of "the prick of conscience" we are using a phrase that expresses the literal meaning of the word *compunction*. The Latin *pungere* means "to prick," "to sting," and *compunctio* means "pricking," "stinging." From this is derived English *compunction* to denote the emotion of remorse with its pricking of the conscience.

Congregation: *a flock*

The symbolism so beautifully expressed in David's twenty-third Psalm is fully justified by the origins of our words *congregation* and *pastor*.

Latin *grex, gregis*, means "flock" or "herd" and is the basis for the word *congregare*, meaning "to gather into a flock." Derived from this is the Latin *congregatio*, which is taken into English as *congregation*. The word *pastor* carries out the same symbolism. Latin *pascere* means "to pasture," "to feed." The past participle *pastum* gives Latin *pastor*, "a shepherd" or "one who has the care of flocks." Later, the figurative meaning developed, "a keeper of souls" or "minister of the church." The two words, therefore, preserve the symbolism of the shepherd and his flock as applied to the *pastor* and his *congregation*.

Congregation

Constable: *originally, count of the stable*

The official title *Constable* has had a strange history and a variety of meanings. It goes back to an original source that has little connection with its present-day meaning. Latin *comes, comitis,* means "companion," and acquires the sense of "king's companion," "thane," "count." Latin *stabulum* means "stable." *Comes stabuli* thus means "thane of the stable," "master of the horse," a position of importance and honor in the early Middle Ages (as indicated also by the history of the word *chivalry*). *Comes stabuli* becomes Old French *conestable,* borrowed in Middle English and giving English *constable.* The chief groom of the stable became the chief officer of the household, of the army, even of the kingdom itself. In Modern English the word has lost its former dignity, now designating a petty officer of local government.

Curfew: *cover the fire for the night*

In the Middle Ages, peasants were required to cover or to extinguish their fires at a fixed hour in the evening, announced by the ringing of a bell called the "cover-fire," French *couvre-feu.* The Norman French used the word in England, where it was adopted as *curfu,* modern *curfew,*

Curfew

meaning the hour and the signal for citizens to retire to their homes, or, as now, for the closing of a public place or the cessation of an activity for the night.

Defalcate: *from the sickle of the Roman farmer*

Latin *falx, falcis,* means "sickle." Combined with *de,* "from," "away," it formed *defalcare,* meaning originally "to cut off with a sickle." A figurative use of this word took on the sense "to deduct," the meaning of the English derivative *defalcate:* "to cut off," "to take away or deduct a part of," used chiefly of money, accounts, rents, income, and the like. In modern use the word has acquired the added sense "to take away, deduct (money) *for one's own purposes,*" that is, "to embezzle money held in trust."

Deliberate: *weighed in the scales*

A *deliberate* decision is one based upon a weighing of the facts and arguments involved—and that is the literal meaning of the word. *Deliberate* is derived from Latin *deliberatus,* past participle of the verb *deliberare,* from *librare,* "to weigh." *Librare* comes from *libra,* "a balance" or "pair of scales."

Defalcate

Delirium: *off the track*

The wandering of the mind that characterizes *delirium* determined the formation of the word. When we trace *delirium* back to its source we find that it comes from Latin *de*, "from," and *lira*, "furrow" or "track." From these two words the Romans formed *delirare*, which properly meant "to go out of the furrow in plowing" but which was applied figuratively to mean "to wander mentally," "to rave." *Delirium*, the Latin word derived from *delirare*, was taken in the same form into English.

Easel: *the artist's donkey*

The names of animals are often appropriated to designate inanimate devices. So a long-necked machine is called a *crane*; an iron affair that stands firm to hold burning logs is a fire*dog* in English and a fire *buck* in German; a large support for almost anything is a *horse*; and a small stand or support, as for an artist's canvas, was called a *donkey*, an *ass*, by the Dutch, whose improvements in the technique of oil painting in the Renaissance made them famous throughout the civilized world. The Dutch word *ezel*, "ass," ultimately from Latin *asinus*, "ass," was taken into English as *easel* in the Dutch metaphorical sense "stand for an artist's canvas."

Deliberate

Eliminate: *to put from one's threshold*

Latin *limen* means "threshold" and *e* (or *ex*) means "out." Combined they form the Latin verb *eliminare*, properly "to put outside the threshold," hence "to expel." The past participle *eliminatus* gives us our English word *eliminate* which earlier had the original, literal meaning "to put out of doors," then "to give out (information)," "to divulge," "to make known," and also "to set at liberty," "release." These meanings are now obsolete, leaving in modern usage only the more primitive significance "to get rid of, as by expulsion."

From the same source (Latin *limen*) we have *preliminary*, literally "before the threshold," now in a figurative sense, "introductory."

Enchant: *from the witch's song*

To be *enchanted*, in the modern sense of the word, is to be delighted or charmed in a high degree—something very different from the original meaning of the word. *Enchant* is ultimately from Latin *cantare*, "to chant," "recite," from *canere*, "to sing." A derivative is *incantare*, "to chant or utter a magic formula over, or against one," "to bewitch." This became French *enchanter*, which English borrowed as *enchant*. The first meaning of the word in English was close to the original

Enchant

sense—"to act on by charms or sorcery," but *enchant* is now also used figuratively to mean "to enrapture," "to charm," as with music, beauty, and the like.

Bewitch is another word that has risen above its original suggestion of evil sorcery, and now means "to fascinate with something delightful."

Charm, also, from French *charme*, in turn from Latin *carmen*, "a song" or "an incantation," has taken on a happier meaning, having drifted away from its early magic sense. A *charming* woman no longer wields her power through incantations!

Enthrall: *literally, to enslave*

Enthrall presents another case of a word the original and literal sense of which is cruel, but the modern, figurative use of which is much more pleasant. When we say that we are *enthralled* by a song, or a book, or something else with captivating charm, it is interesting to remember that the original meaning of the word was "to enslave." *Thrall* is Anglo-Saxon for "slave." To *enthrall* meant, therefore, "to enslave," "to reduce to the condition of a thrall." The literal sense of "enslave," "make captive," easily yields a figurative sense, "captivate the senses," "hold spellbound," "charm," as with a song or a story.

Enthrall

Enthusiasm: *religious frenzy*

Greek *theos* means "god," *entheos* or *enthous* means "having a god within," "possessed by a god," "inspired," and *enthousiasmos*, "divine possession," "ecstasy." The English word *enthusiasm* first meant "inspiration as if by a divine or superhuman power," then "exaltation of soul," "zeal," "fervor," and, finally, also the thing that excites zeal or fervor.

Escape: *to slip out of one's cape*

The word *escape* gives us a picture of a prisoner, held by his cape or coat, who suddenly slips out of the garment and flees. The word *escape* comes from Old (North) French *escaper* (French *échapper*), made from a Late Latin phrase *ex cappa*, "out of one's cape or cloak."

Exaggerate: *literally, to heap up*

When one tells a story with a good bit of exaggeration, he is, in the colloquial phrase, "piling it on," which comes very close to translating the word *exaggerate*. This is derived from Latin *exaggerare*, "to heap up," an intensive form of *aggerare*, "to bring to," "bring on," from *ad*, "to," and *gerere*, "to bear," "bring." Its first English meaning was also "to heap up," "to accumulate," but this sense has disappeared, leaving the figurative one, "to enlarge beyond bounds or truth," "to overstate."

Expedite: *to free the foot*

Latin *expedire* is a compound of *ex*, "out," and *pes*, *pedis*, "foot," and means "to free one caught by the foot," "to extricate." Its past participle *expeditus* is the source of English *expedite*, the original meaning of which was "to relieve of impediments," "to set free," then, figuratively, "to accelerate the process or progress of anything," "to facilitate."

Extravagant: *wandering out of bounds*

An *extravagant* man goes beyond the bounds of reason in his expenditures, in his talk, and so on. *Extravagant* is derived from Latin *extra*, "on the outside," combined with *vagans*, "wandering," from *vagus*, "vague," "wandering." The first meaning in English was literal—"wandering beyond one's bounds," "roving," but the word is now used figuratively: "out of bounds in speech or conduct."

Fee: *tribute in money, once reckoned in terms of cattle*

Thirty centuries ago, the ancestors of the present peoples of Europe, the Indo-Europeans, were nomadic herdsmen whose medium of exchange was their cattle. So the word for "cattle" meant also "money": Latin *pecus*, "cattle," gives *pecunia*, "property," "money"; Anglo-Saxon *feoh* means both "cattle" and "property," "money." From a continental Teutonic language akin to Anglo-Saxon, the French borrowed this word, making Old French *fieu* or *fié*, taken into Middle English as *fe*, meaning "fief" and "payment." Both meanings are still current: "fief" in the legal phrases "hold in *fee*" and "*fee* simple"; and "payment," "tribute," in the *fee* paid for occasional services, as to a physician, a lawyer, or the like.

Fool: *a bellows, a windbag*

Latin *follis* means "a bellows," "a windbag." This became Old French *fol*, "a foolish person," just as we to-day say "a windbag." Middle English borrowed the word in the same form, *fol*, giving Modern English *fool*.

Free: *the loved ones of the household*

The root of the word *free* meant originally "love": Gothic *frijōn*, "to love," akin to Sanskrit *priya*, "beloved." The primitive household included the master's family (related by blood or by marriage) and also the slaves. The members of the family were the "loved ones," as we still call them, the *free*, as distinct from the slaves. So the word *free*, "beloved," came to mean "not slave," "free" in our modern sense.

Garret: *once a place for a lookout*

A place of lookout atop a building was called in Old French *garite*, after the verb *garir*, "to preserve," "to defend." The word passed into Middle English with the same meaning, "turret," "watchtower," "place of lookout"; and, as the need for keeping such lookouts lessened, *garret* came to mean merely the topmost part of a house, where the lookout used to be, immediately under the roof.

Gossip: *a sponsor in baptism*

The word *gossip* has sadly degenerated in meaning. It originally denoted a person bound to another by a religious ceremony, especially a sponsor in baptism—Anglo-Saxon *godsibb*, from *god*, "God," and *sib*, "related," "a relation." From this came Middle English *gossib*, modern *gossip*. The first meanings, "sponsor," "godfather or godmother," are obsolete. A more general sense developed, "companion," "familiar acquaintance," especially a talkative one, hence, "a newsmonger"; and finally, *gossip* means "the talk, tattle, of a gossip," "idle talk," "rumor."

Grog: *named for its originator*

Admiral Vernon was known to the English navy in the eighteenth century as "Old Grog," from the *grogram* cloak which he wore in foul weather. He became still more famous for his order, issued about 1740, to water the rum rationed out to the sailors. This dilute mixture was promptly dubbed *grog* after its originator, and the word has since been applied to intoxicating liquors in general.

Gymnasium: *no longer in its literal meaning*

In the golden age of Athens, athletics played an important part in Greek life, and physical strength and grace were highly regarded. The athletes, in their games, were not impeded by costumes;

they exercised nude. "Nude" in Greek is *gymnos*. The derivative *gymnazein* means "to exercise (nude)." A *gymnasion* was a "place where athletic exercises were performed (in the nude)." This is the source of our own word *gymnasium*, which has retained the sense of activity if not that of costume.

Halcyon: *a bird that calmed the waves*

The ancients believed that the kingfisher (in Greek, *halkyōn*) built a floating nest on the sea at the winter solstice and magically calmed the waves during its nesting time. The fable accounted for a succession of calm days supposed to occur annually at this period (called the *halcyon* days). So any serene, peaceful period is called "*halcyon* days."

Harangue: *addressed to a ring of people*

Teutonic *hring*, "ring," "circle," as, for instance, a circle of hearers listening to a speech, was borrowed by the Gauls; but the harsh Teutonic *hr-* was hard to pronounce, and gave *har-*, as in French *harangue*. The meaning is no longer the "audience" but the "speech," the *harangue*.

Hazard: *from the old game of chance*

The Spanish word *azar* means "an unforeseen disaster," "an unfortunate card or throw at dice." Through the French form *hasard*, it came into English as *hazard*, originally a game of chance played with dice, a simplified form of which is modern craps. The meaning broadened into "the uncertain result of throwing a die," hence "a chance," "an accident," and the still more general "risk," "danger."

Hearse: *originally, a harrow*

The Latin *hirpex* means "harrow," an agricultural implement, usually triangular, set with teeth and drawn over plowed land to level it and break the clods. Latin *hirpex* became Old French *herce*, Middle English *herse*, and Modern English *hearse*. The triangular frame bearing candles, used at Tenebrae in Holy Week, was called *hearse* because of its triangular shape, and because the projecting candles suggested the teeth of the harrow. By extension, *hearse* came to mean also a framework bearing candles under which the coffin was set during funeral ceremonies, and then a framework to cover a coffin; then "monument," "grave"; then "bier," or "handbarrow for conveying the dead to the grave"; eventually, a carriage, and now, at last, a motor van, used for conveying the coffin.

Humble: *literally, on the ground*

Humus in Latin means "earth," "ground," and the derived adjective *humilis* means "on the ground," "low." Latin *humilis* became French *humble*, which was taken into English. *Humble* is now more commonly figurative: "thinking lowly of one's self."

Humiliate is also derived from the same Latin *humilis* and means, literally, "to put on the ground," hence "to humble."

Humor: *a fluid of medieval physiology*

Humor is Latin for "moisture," "fluid," and our English word at first retained the same meaning. In old physiology the *humors* were the four fluids (blood, phlegm, choler, and melancholy) conceived as entering into the constitution of the body and determining by their relative proportions the individual's health and temperament. Something of this meaning survives in medical use, but in popular use *humor* has come to mean "disposition" or "state of mind," as in "good humor," "ill humor," and the like. More especially, *humor* has come to signify one particular side of one's temperament—the mental faculty of discovering, expressing, or appreciating the ludicrous—and the word has broadened to cover also that quality in anything that appeals to the sense of humor. There is an interesting comparison to be made with the word *complexion*.

Impediment: *entanglement of the feet*

Here is a word which, in its literal meaning, refers to the feet, but which in modern use refers also to the tongue. We speak of a person who is tongue-tied as suffering from an *impediment* of speech, but *impediment* is derived from a Latin word meaning originally an "entanglement of the feet." Latin *pes, pedis*, means "foot"; the derived verb *impedire* means "to entangle the feet," "to impede," "to hinder"; and the noun *impedimentum* means "entanglement," "hindrance," or, in the plural, *impedimenta*, "baggage." From this word is derived English *impediment*, meaning "obstruction," broadened so that it denotes anything that obstructs, even an organic obstruction to speech.

Inaugurate

Inaugurate: *the taking of omens*

When we speak of the *inauguration* of a president we use a word that carries us back to ancient times when people believed in omens and looked for them on every important occasion. Latin *augur* meant a member of the highest class of official diviners of ancient Rome, whose duty it was to observe and interpret the omens, such as the flight of birds, at the time of any important event. *Inaugurare* meant "to take omens" before entering upon a critical undertaking, such as the proclamation of an emperor. From the past participle *inauguratus* is derived English *inaugurate*, though the ceremony of *inauguration* to-day does not call for the observation of omens.

Incisive: *cutting like a chisel*

When you apply the word *incisive* to speaking, writing, or thinking, do you realize that you are using a word that pictures a sharp cutting instrument? The Latin *in*, "in," and *caedere*, "to cut," were combined to form the verb *incidere*, meaning "to cut into." From the past participle of this verb comes our English verb *incise*, with the same meaning, as well as our adjective *incisive*, applied to thinking that is acute and expression that cuts clean and penetrates. The *incisive* speech of such

Incisive

an orator as Theodore Roosevelt was a keen-edged tool for cutting his message deeply into the minds of his hearers.

Infant: *one who cannot speak*

Latin *in*, meaning "un-," "not," and *fari*, "to speak," were combined to form *infans*, literally, "not speaking," "a babe." This is the origin of our word *infant. Infantry* comes from the same source. Italian *infante*, meaning first "infant," "child," "boy," came to mean "servant," "squire of a knight," hence "foot soldier." The derivative *infanteria* means "a body of foot soldiers," French *infanterie* and English *infantry*.

Insect: *with a body that is cut in*

In popular usage, an *insect* is any of numerous small invertebrate animals generally having the body more or less obviously segmented. This segmentation gives the body the appearance of being cut in, or almost divided, and it is this characteristic that gives the *insect* its name, derived from Latin *insectus*, past participle of *insecare*, "to cut in."

Entomology, the word meaning the department of zoölogy that treats of insects, is derived from

Greek words which translate Latin *insectum*. *Entomology* is derived from Greek *entomon*, "insect," from *entomos*, "cut in," from *en*, "in," and a form of the root of *temnein*, "to cut," referring, just like the word *insect*, to the fact that the insect appears to be nearly cut in two.

Instill: *drop by drop*

That gradual imparting of anything such as wisdom, virtue, love, which is implied in our word *instill* can be very clearly understood when we consider the source of the word. *Instill* comes from Latin *stilla*, meaning "a drop," giving the verb *stillare*, "to drop," and the derivative compound *instillare*, "to pour in, drop by drop." This literal meaning of *instill* has given place to the figurative one of gradually imparting qualities of heart and mind.

Distill* also is derived from Latin *stilla*, in this case combined with *de*, "down," to form *distillare*, "to let fall in drops."

Insult: *literally, to leap upon*

The phrase "to jump on," signifying to reprimand severely or to treat with discourtesy, may be slang, but, like many another popular expression, it makes graphic use of a metaphor in good standing etymologically. Its meaning is closely allied to that of the word *insult*, and *insult* comes from a Latin verb *insultare*, from *insilire*, "to leap on," a compound of *salire*, "to leap." The first meaning of *insult* in English was "to make an attack upon," specifically in a military sense. That meaning is obsolete and *insult* is restricted to a figurative use with the sense of offering a wanton affront.

Intoxicate: *from the poisoned arrows of ancient bowmen*

Those who speak of intoxicating liquor as "poison" may quote, as their justification, the literal meaning of the word, as well as its original use in English. The Greek word *toxon* means "bow" or "arrow." From this was derived the Greek *toxicon* (borrowed in Latin as *toxicum*), "a poison in which arrows were dipped." This was the source of the Latin *intoxicare*, "to drug or poison," the past participle of which gave English *intoxicate* with the same meaning. This sense "to poison" is retained, or revived, only in a special medical sense in *auto-intoxication*, literally, "self-poisoning," signifying poisoning from toxic substances produced in the body. *Toxic, toxin*, and other medical terms coming from the same source also retain the original significance of "poison." In ordinary use the word *intoxicate* has been narrowed to the meaning "overstimulate," as with strong drink or with great emotion.

Intoxicate

Investigate: *to follow the footprints*

In Latin, *vestigium* means "footprint," and *vestigare* "to track or trace by footprints." In the form *investigare* the meaning shifted from literal to figurative, and instead of "tracking men or animals by their footprints" it meant "tracing facts or searching for information." From this source comes English *investigate*.

Vestigium has given us also *vestige*, the first meaning of which was, as in Latin, "footprint," but which has come to mean "a trace or visible sign" left by something lost, perished, or gone.

Journey: *a day's travel*

Latin *dies* means "day," and *diurnus* "belonging to the day." This is the origin of the Old French *jorn*, "a day," and *jornée*, "a day's work," "a day's travel." Middle English borrowed this as *jornee*, *journee*, "a day's travel." The modern form *journey* now refers to travel without regard to the time consumed. From French *journal*—from Latin *diurnalis*, "diurnal," a derivative of *diurnus*—we have our word *journal*, "a diary or daybook," then a "newspaper" or other periodical publication.

Lace: *made with a noose*

It is strange to think of a delicate piece of Chantilly *lace* being connected with the snare of the ancient Romans. Yet, etymologically, the word *lace* has its origin in Latin *laqueus*, "noose" or "snare." *Laqueus* gave Old French *laz*, borrowed into Middle English as *las*, Modern English *lace*. *Lace* at first retained the meaning of its Latin original, "noose," "snare," or "net." Then it meant simply the cord itself, especially a cord that holds by being tied or interwoven (for instance, shoe *lace*). Eventually, *lace* was applied to an openwork fabric of laced or interwoven threads.

Libel: *merely an innocent little book*

In ancient times the inner bark (Latin *liber*) of certain trees served as material on which to write. *Liber* came thus to mean also "paper" and "book." The diminutive form *libellus* meant "little book," "pamphlet." English *libel* is from this source. Since pamphlets and handbills were used to disseminate unfavorable and scandalous reports about rivals and enemies, the word *libel* took on the meaning "lampoon," "defamatory statement."

Libertine: *suggesting an abuse of liberty*

Latin *liber* means "free." From *liber* was derived *libertus*, "one made free," and *libertinus*, "a freed-man," "a freed slave." From *libertinus* English made the word *libertine*. Since the morals of ex-slaves were notorious, *libertine* suggested loose conduct, and from this suggestion came the modern sense "debauchee," one whose liberty has become license.

Magazine: *a storehouse of information or entertainment*

Magazine, the word by which we designate a pamphlet published periodically containing stories, articles, and the like, goes back for its origin to an Arabic word *makhzan*, meaning a "storehouse," "granary," or "cellar." Arabic *makhzan* was borrowed by Spanish as *magacén*, and this by French as *magasin*, English *magazine*, meaning first "storehouse or depot," especially for military stores. Then the sense was extended to a "storehouse of information," originally in the form of a book, but now any periodical publication.

Mail: *originally, the postman's bag*

Mail is to-day a broad word meaning not only the letters and other things which come through the post office, but also the whole system of conveyance and delivery of postal matter. It is interesting to find that this great system is designated by a term which originally meant simply the bag in which letters were carried. *Mail* in this sense has nothing to do with *mail*, "metal mesh," used as body armor in the Middle Ages (shirt of *mail*). Our present *mail* was Middle English *male*, from Old French *male* (modern French *malle*), "bag," "trunk," which came from an old Teutonic form *malaha* or *malha*, "wallet."

Manufacture: *literally, a making by hand*

The modern sense of *manufacture* is the contradiction of its original sense, for *manufacture* comes from Latin *manus*, "hand," and *facere*, "to make," that is, "a making by hand." The development of modern industry has carried the word along with the process which it named. Things are no longer made by hand, or almost never. *Manufacture* now suggests machinery and our word *hand-made* must now be used to convey the literal sense of *manufacture*.

Marmalade: *a preserve of honey apple (quince)*

The Greek *meli*, "honey," and *mēlon*, "apple," were combined into *melimēlon*, "a sweet apple," "an apple grafted on a quince." Latin borrowed it as *melimelum*, which became Portuguese *marmelo*, "quince." *Marmelada* is "a preserve of *marmelo*." French *marmelade* and English *marmalade* are borrowed from the Portuguese.

Melancholy: *from the black bile supposed to cause it*

In the history of the word *humor* we found that, according to ancient physiology, there were four body fluids that determined a person's health and temperament. One of these four was black bile, an excess of which was thought to be the cause of gloominess and ill nature. This was called in Greek *melancholia*—from *melas* (stem *melan-*), "black," and *cholē*, "bile." Through the Latin form *melancholia* and Old French *melancolie*, the word came into English, now spelled *melancholy*. Its original meaning "black bile" is now obsolete with the physiology that invented it. But the gloomy mood remains, and is still called *melancholy*, after the black bile that was supposed to be its cause.

Milliner: *a man from Milan*

Milliner was originally *Milaner*, simply "an inhabitant of Milan" or "a man from Milan," more particularly, one who imported women's finery. To-day the *milliner* is primarily a dealer in women's hats.

Monster: *an omen of misfortune*

Monstrum is Latin for "a divine omen of misfortune." It is connected with *monstrare*, "to point out." Old French and Middle English borrowed *monstrum* as *monstre*, Modern English *monster*, meaning first "a marvel," "something extraordinary," then "a fabulous animal," "an unnatural creature," any huge or enormous animal or thing, and also anything monstrous, especially a person of unnatural or excessive ugliness, deformity, wickedness, or cruelty.

Neighbor: *once a near-by farmer*

Neighbor is one of those interesting words that carry us back to Anglo-Saxon days. In Anglo-Saxon, *néah* meant "nigh," "near," and *gebūr* meant "dweller," "farmer." These two words were combined into *néahgebūr*, meaning, literally, "a near-by farmer." The word appears in Medieval English in the

Neighbor

form *neighebour* and in Modern English as *neighbor*. Its meaning, changing with the evolution of civilization, no longer applies particularly to neighboring farmers but refers to persons living near each other in apartment house suites or suburban cottages as well as to those on near-by farms. Even nations in the modern world are called "neighbors"—an interesting development of a word that means, literally, "near-by farmers."

Opportune: *at the port*

Latin *portus*, "port," "harbor," with the preposition *ob*, "at" or "before," formed *opportunus*, literally, "at the port," but used figuratively to mean "ready," "convenient." From this source we have our word *opportune*, meaning "fit," "suitable," "timely," and *opportunity*, "a favorable time," or, more broadly, "a suitable combination of conditions."

Orchestra: *the place for the chorus of dancers*

Our word *orchestra* is derived from a Greek word meaning "to dance"—*orcheisthai*. From this word, the Greeks formed *orchēstra*, meaning "the place for the chorus of dancers," which was a circular area in front of the stage in the Greek theater. The Romans used the word to designate a corresponding semicircular space where persons of distinction had their seats. English borrowed the word to denote the space occupied by a band of instrumental performers, commonly just in front of the stage, and also to denote the band itself. By extension, *orchestra* came to mean the forward part, or all, of the main floor of a theater.

Panic: *from the mischievous god of the ancient Greeks*

In Greek mythology there was no greater trouble maker among the pagan deities than Pan. His abrupt appearance among the timid wood nymphs inspired frantic efforts to escape. He was suspected also of inspiring human beings with unreasonable terror. So the Greeks imagined that sudden, contagious fear which seemed to have no sufficient cause must have been inspired by Pan, and to denote this fear they created from the name of this dreaded god the word *panicos*. Modern English has taken the word in the form *panic*, and although *panics* are staged in such modern settings as Wall Street instead of in a primitive forest, the word still suggests a terror-stricken stampede caused by fear that has no apparent grounds.

Pariah

L. SZANTO

Parasite: *eating at the table of another*

Among the Greeks and Romans there was a class of men who made themselves welcome at the houses of rich men by providing flattering entertainment, especially at meals. The Greeks called such a man *parasitos*, from *para*, "beside," and *sitos*, "wheat," "grain," or "food." Thus the word meant one "eating beside" another, and hence, one who, without doing useful work himself, manages to be supported by another. Latin borrowed the word as *parasitus*, and English as *parasite*. Its first meaning was close to the original Greek sense, but it came to be applied, in biology, to a plant or animal living in, on, or with some other living organism at whose expense it obtains its food, shelter, or some other advantage.

Pariah: *a drum beater in India*

In the complicated caste system of India, certain occupations and functions are assigned to particular castes. Members of one of the lowest castes, according to traditional usage, were hired to beat drums at certain festivals, and so were called the "drum beaters" (Tamil *paraiyan*, "drummer," from *parai*, a sort of drum). We have borrowed the name of the caste as *pariah*, but not the strict sense: in English a *pariah* is any despised person, an outcast.

Pavilion

Pavilion: *from a butterfly*

The Latin word *papilio* means "butterfly," and hence also an awning or tent, stretched out like a butterfly's wings. From *papilio* came French *pavillon*, borrowed by Middle English as *pavilon*, Modern English *pavilion*, now usually a shelter more permanent than a tent.

Pecuniary: *from the barter of primitive herdsmen*

In the nomadic period of Indo-European civilization, before money in precious metal or other compact symbols was thought of, a man's wealth was reckoned in flocks and herds. Latin *pecus* means "cattle," and the derivative *pecunia* meant, originally, "property in cattle." As civilization advanced and wealth was represented by many things other than cattle, the old word was kept for the broader new meaning. When money was invented and adopted as a measurement of wealth, the word *pecunia* took on the new meaning "money." Derived from this was the adjective *pecuniarius*, "relating to or consisting of money," from which we made English *pecuniary*.

Note the interesting comparison to be made with English *fee*: Latin *pecu-s* and primitive Teutonic *fehu* are the same word, *p* having become *f* and *c* (*k*) having become *h* in Teutonic. Refer to the definition of *Grimm's Law* in Webster's New International Dictionary.

Pecuniary

Pedagogue: *a slave in ancient Greece*

The rich man of ancient Greece numbered among his slaves one who was particularly charged with the care of the master's sons in their youth. One of the duties of this slave was to escort the boys to and from school. The Greek words *pais, paidos,* "boy," and *agōgos,* "leading or guiding," formed *paidagōgos,* literally, "boy-guiding." Latin borrowed this as *paedagogus,* French as *pédagogue,* and English as *pedagogue.* During this evolution, the attendant became the tutor and, eventually, the teacher in the classroom, but still retained the same name.

Pedigree: *like the footprint of a crane*

Imagine a genealogist of the Middle Ages tracing the history of a family back to some early ancestor. To picture the record graphically he makes a drawing showing the original stock and the various families and descendants branching from it. Noticing that the shape of his drawing suggests the footprint of a large bird, he dubs his record *pied de grue,* French for "crane's foot." Middle English adapted the phrase to *pedegru* and, since French *u* is pronounced very nearly like English *ee,* Modern English spelled it *pedigree.* In common use it is now more frequently applied to

Pedagogue

L.SZANTO

the lineage of a highly bred animal, such as a horse or a dog. Our own phrase "family tree" is an example of another metaphor applied to the branching lines of a genealogy.

Pencil: *from a little tail*

The Latin *penicillus*, meaning "a little tail," is the ancestor of our word *pencil*. The term *pencil* was first applied to a brush of hair or bristles used by artists and suggestive, in its form, of the "little tail" from which it was named. Later, the word took on its present common meaning.

Pen is derived from Latin *penna*, meaning "feather." This is natural enough, because the first pens were feathers or quills. When the quill pen gave way to the modern instrument of steel or gold the name remained to remind us of a custom of earlier days.

Precipitate: *headfirst*

When we think of a *precipitate* action we have a picture of a person dashing headlong into something. This picture is true, etymologically, for *precipitate* means, literally, "headfirst." It comes from Latin *prae*, "before," and *caput*, "head."

Precipitate

Precipice has the same origin, but through French *précipice*, from Latin *praecipitium*, "a headlong fall," hence, a place from which one might fall headlong, "a steep cliff."

Precocious: *cooked beforehand*

Latin *prae*, "before," and *coquere*, "to cook," were combined to form *praecoquere*, "to cook beforehand" or "to ripen beforehand," in the latter sense applied to fruits ripened early. From this was derived English *precocious*, originally applied to plants and trees with the meaning "flowering or fruiting early or before the usual time," "early or prematurely ripe or developed." It was only a step to the metaphorical application of the word to children of premature development.

Preposterous: *suggesting our idiom "the cart before the horse"*

Latin *praeposterus* is a combination of *prae*, "before," and *posterus*, "latter." Its first meaning in English was the same as the Latin—"having that first which ought to be last," "inverted in order," hence, "illogical," "contrary to nature, reason, or common sense," "ridiculous."

Pretext: *having a curtain of deception*

Latin *texere* means "to weave" and *prae* means "before"; they were combined to form *praetexere*, literally meaning "to weave before." The past participle *praetextus*, "woven before," was applied to a curtain; hence, the noun *praetextum* meant "concealment," or, figuratively, "concealment of the truth." French *prétexte* and English *pretext* are borrowed from Latin *praetextum*. We use the metaphor "smoke screen" in a similar sense.

Prevaricate: *from crooked walk to crooked talk*

Prevaricate shows an interesting evolution from literal to figurative meaning. Its history starts with Latin *varus*, "bent," with the derivatives *varicus*, "straddling," and *varicare*, "to straddle." Combining *prae*, "before," with *varicare*, the Romans formed *praevaricari*, the primitive meaning of which was "to walk crookedly." The past participle *praevaricatus* was borrowed in English as *prevaricate*, meaning "to deviate," "to go astray," "to deviate from the truth."

Procrastinate: *to put off till to-morrow*

The poet says: "Procrastination is the thief of time." The man in the street says: "Never put off till to-morrow what you can do to-day." The expressions are seemingly different, but the interesting thing about them is that *procrastination* and *putting off till to-morrow* have exactly the same literal meaning. The word *procrastinate* originated in the Latin word *cras*, which means "to-morrow." *Crastinus*, "of to-morrow," was combined with *pro*, "forward," to form *procrastinare*, literally, "to put forward to to-morrow" or "to put off till to-morrow," and its past participle *procrastinatus* was adapted to make English *procrastinate*.

Psalm: *from the Greek musician's harp*

Greek *psallein* meant first "to pull," "to twitch," and then, applied specifically, "to play upon a stringed instrument," as a harp, then "to sing to the harp." The verb *psallein* formed a noun *psalmos*, "a song or poem," "a sacred song." Borrowed by Latin as *psalmus*, it gave Anglo-Saxon and Middle English *salm*. Modern English still pronounces the word so, but the Latin spelling *psalm* has been restored.

Rapture: *formerly, abduction*

The extreme joy or pleasure denoted by our word *rapture* represents a strange, though logical,

Psalm

L. SZANTO

evolution from the original meaning of the word. *Rapture* originated in Latin *rapere* (past participle, *raptus*), "to carry off by force," and the first meaning in English was the same, or, in a specific sense, "abduction." Then *rapture* was applied to the mental condition of being "carried away by excitement" in both an agreeable and a disagreeable sense. In modern use, the word is restricted to the meaning "carried away by joy."

Recalcitrant: *like a kicking mule*

Our phrase "kicking over the traces" makes use of a metaphor very similar to that found in the history of the word *recalcitrant*. From Latin *calx*, "heel," was formed *calcitrare*, "to kick," and *recalcitrare*, "to kick back," with a participle *recalcitrans* (stem *recalcitrant-*), "kicking back." This is the source of English *recalcitrant*, literally, "kicking back," hence "refractory," "obstinate," now applied to human beings as well as to mules or horses.

Record: *literally, to learn by heart*

Nowadays we *record* facts and preserve the story of events by committing them to writing or

Recalcitrant

L. SZANTO.

by incorporating them in some tangible form. But the word *record* itself is a reminder of a more primitive way: learning things "by heart." *Record* is derived from Latin *recordari*, "to remember," formed from *re-*, "again," "back," and *cor* (stem *cord-*), "heart." The earlier English meaning "to get by heart," "to learn, as by repeating," has become obsolete: we "remember" things more reliably by putting them in books.

Rehearse: *to harrow again*

The farmer, after plowing his field, goes over it with a harrow to break up the clods and level the ground. Sometimes, in order to make the field still smoother, he harrows it over again.

Old French *herce* meant "a harrow," *hercier*, "to harrow," and *rehercier*, "to harrow over again," borrowed in Middle English as *rehercen*, Modern English *rehearse*. Now we *rehearse*, not the plowed field, but a speech, a play, or the like. See the story of the word *hearse* for an interesting connection with *rehearse*.

Remorse: *bite again*

That constant gnawing pain which is caused by a sense of guilt, and which we call *remorse*, is

Rehearse

L.SZANTO

well named. For *remorse* goes back to the Latin *remordere*, "to bite again," or "bite back," from *mordere*, "to bite." The Late Latin noun *remorsus* gave Old French and Middle English *remors*, which was, to be sure, literally translated in Middle English *ayenbite*, "again bite"; but the neater Latin word survived in Modern English *remorse*.

Ruminate: *to chew over in the mind*

Cattle grazing in a meadow do not chew thoroughly grass which they crop, but swallow it into a special stomach and bring it back, at a later time, for leisurely mastication. This is the chewing of the cud denoted by the word *ruminate*, a graphic metaphor to designate the bringing back to mind of some matter needing more thorough consideration or reflection, especially in the deeply contemplative manner of the cow chewing her cud. Thus *ruminate* takes on its figurative meaning "to ponder."

Sacrifice: *a thing made sacred*

Latin *sacer*, "sacred," with a combining form of *facere*, "to make," gave *sacrificare*, "to make sacred," "to devote, or offer, to the god." Since this offering generally entailed death to the thing offered,

Sacrifice

and its destruction on the altar, the word came to mean "to kill or destroy." The corresponding Latin noun, *sacrificium*, was borrowed in Old French and Middle English as *sacrifice*.

From the live sacrifice to one's god, it is a far cry to the modern world's "sacrifice sales" and baseball's "sacrifice hits."

Salary: *originally, salt money*

Roman soldiers, as a part of their pay, drew a special allowance originally for the purchase of salt, in ancient times not always so easily obtained as now. The allowance "for salt" was called *salarium*, from *sal*, "salt." The word was later used to mean "pension." Latin *salarium* was borrowed in English as *salary*, "fixed regular wages," but used in connection with civilian workers only, not soldiers. A soldier draws his "pay," not a *salary!*

Sarcophagus: *a flesh eater*

The ancient Greeks used, for the making of coffins, a limestone which disintegrated in a few weeks the flesh of bodies deposited in it. Such a coffin was called *sarkophagos*, literally, "eating flesh," a word formed from *sarx*, "flesh," and *phagein*, "to eat." From this origin comes our word *sarcophagus*, which has lost its literal significance and denotes merely any stone coffin or large coffin placed where it may be seen.

Satan: *the great adversary*

Satan, the Devil of the Scriptures, is man's great enemy—and his very name records this enmity. *Satan* is derived from Hebrew *sātān*, "adversary," which is based upon *sātan*, "to be adverse," "to persecute."

Savage: *forest-dwelling*

Latin *silva*, "a wood," "a forest," makes the adjective *silvaticus*, "belonging to the forest," and hence, "wild." A slightly different pronunciation of this word gave Old French *sauvage*, borrowed in English as *savage*, which now means not only "forest-dwelling" but in general "untamed," "uncultivated," and so "fierce," "brutal."

Season: *originally, the sowing time*

Our word *season*, which to-day may be any of the four divisions of the year, or may, indeed, be

Season

used in most of the general senses of "time," once meant specifically the "sowing time." It goes back to Latin *serere* (past participle, *satum*), "to sow," "to plant," from which was derived *satio*, "a sowing," "a planting." Old French *saison*, which had already the generalized sense of "suitable time," not specifically "sowing time," was borrowed in Middle English as *sesoun*, Modern English *season*, the "time" for almost anything, from opera to oysters.

Seminary: *literally, a seed bed*

In modern use *seminary* denotes a place of education such as a preparatory school, or sometimes a special sort of college. It would be appropriate to say "a place where seeds are planted in the minds of the pupils," because *seminary* is derived from a word meaning "seed." Latin *semen, seminis*, "seed," made the noun *seminarium*, "a nursery" for plants, then a place for raising and training the young. English borrowed this as *seminary*, with the same senses as the Latin.

Senate: *an assembly of the elders*

The minimum age requirement of thirty years for members of the United States *Senate* is something of a contradiction of the original meaning of the word. Latin *senatus*, the supreme council of the state in ancient Rome, is from *senex*, "old man." The *senate* was the council of elders.

On the other hand, *senile*, which is also derived from Latin *senex*, has intensified its significance "aged," and means "feeble with age."

Senior, literally "older," is the comparative adjective of *senex*, "old." Its meaning has broadened to cover superiority, or, as we say, seniority, of rank as well as of years.

Sinister: *the unlucky left*

There is an old superstition that the left side is unlucky and that anything appearing or observed on the left is inauspicious. The Latin word *sinister* means "left," "on the left hand," hence, "awkward," and also "unlucky," "bad," and so forth. It was borrowed in English in the same form and with the same meanings.

Slogan: *a war cry of the clan*

Among the Highland clans of Scotland the war cry, or gathering word, was called *sluagh-ghairm*, a Gaelic term formed from *sluagh*, "army," and *gairm*, "a call." The English form *slogan* took on the meaning "any rallying or battle cry" and in modern use has come to be applied to business mottoes far from its original warlike significance.

Steward: *the sty warden*

Anglo-Saxon *stigu*, "sty," "pigpen," and *weard*, "guard," "warden," combined into *stīweard*, literally, "sty warden." In feudal times in England the word (Middle English *stiward*) came to denote a household officer having charge of cattle, and later the head manager of a manor or estate. It came into Modern English as *steward*, a term applied to positions very different from those denoted by its earlier meaning.

Stigma: *from an ancient branding iron*

It was the custom among the ancients to place upon slaves, criminals, and soldiers an identifying mark, called, in Greek, *stigma*, from *stizein*, "to prick," "to brand." Latin borrowed the word in the same form to mean "a mark made with a burning iron," "a brand," and figuratively, any mark of infamy or disgrace, a stain or reproach caused by dishonorable conduct. It is borrowed in English with all these senses.

Stirrup: *a mounting rope*

The *stirrup* of a saddle to-day is used in riding as well as in mounting. That its original purpose was primarily as an aid in mounting is suggested in the history of the word. *Stirrup*, Middle English *stirop*, is from Anglo-Saxon *stigrāp*, from *stīgan*, "to ascend," and *rāp*, "a rope." *Stirrup* was therefore originally a loop of rope into which one stepped in mounting a horse.

Stoic: *from the "Painted Porch" in Athens*

In the fourth century B.C., a school of philosophy was founded in Athens by Zeno, who taught in the market place of Athens, in a portico that was called the "Painted Porch." In Greek, *stoa* means "a roofed colonnade," "a porch," and *stōikos*, "pertaining to a colonnade." This word, identifying the place of their meetings, became the name of Zeno's school of philosophy. Zeno taught that the wise man should be free from passion, unsubdued by joy or grief, willingly submissive to natural law; hence, "a stoic" came to mean one not easily excited, one apparently or professedly indifferent to pleasure or pain. Latin borrowed *stōikos* as *stoicus*, whence English *stoic*.

Subtle: *from the ancient weaver at his loom*

The Latin word *subtilis*, meaning "woven fine," was applied to delicate fabrics. Its direct descendant is our word *subtle*, which first meant "tenuous," "delicate," but which has shifted to mean "skillfully or cunningly devised." A "*subtle* answer" therefore is one that is "finely woven," or, in other words, cleverly and delicately presented.

Succinct: *literally, tucked up*

The Latin *cingere* means "to gird." With the prefix *sub*, "under," it forms *succingere*, "to gird below or from below," "to tuck up." The form *succinctus* means "girded or tucked up," with reference to clothing, and that was the first meaning of the English derivative *succinct*. This sense is now archaic. The present sense is metaphorical, applied to statements that are, as it were, "tucked in," that is, "concise," "terse."

Supercilious: *the eyebrows expressing arrogance*

In Latin, *super*, "over," plus *cilium*, "eyelid," formed *supercilium*, meaning "eyebrow." Because raising the eyebrows is a characteristic habit of the haughty man, *supercilium* came to mean "pride,"

LOUIS SZANTO

and *superciliosus*, "eyebrow-ish," came to mean "haughty," "arrogant." Directly from this Latin word comes our word *supercilious*, giving those who know its origin a mental picture of the eyebrows raised in disdain.

Superfluous: *flowing over*

To express the idea of something being in excess of what is wanted, English borrowed an effective metaphor from the Latin. *Superfluous* is derived from Latin *superfluus*, "overflowing," a word which comes from *super*, "over," and *fluere*, "to flow."

Symposium: *a drinking party*

A *symposium*, the collected opinions of a number of persons on a single subject, means, literally, "a drinking together." The word is Latin, borrowed from Greek *symposion*, from *syn*, "with," "together," and *posis*, "a drinking." A *symposion* was a convivial occasion, with general conversation, such, for instance, as was imagined and reported in Plato's dialogue entitled *The Symposium*, where the guests discuss a philosophical question; hence, any similar report or collection of remarks was called a *symposium*.

Tally

Tally: *a reminder of the early method of counting*

Tally goes back to the time when things were commonly counted by cutting notches in a stick of wood. The word was borrowed in Middle English as *taille*, from Old French *taille*, "a cutting," and also "a tally," connected with French *tailler*, "to cut." It was formerly customary for traders to have two sticks and to mark with notches on each the number or quantity of goods delivered, the seller keeping one stick and the purchaser the other. When such records came to be kept on paper, the same word was used for them; and it now means almost any kind of count or score.

Tantalize: *to torment with the punishment of Tantalus*

In Greek mythology King Tantalus offended the gods and was punished in an extraordinary manner. He was placed in the midst of a lake whose waters reached his chin but receded whenever he attempted to allay his thirst. Over his head hung branches laden with choice fruit, which likewise receded whenever he stretched out his hand to satisfy his hunger. Tantalus became the symbol of such teasing, and his name is the root of our verb *tantalize*.

Tantalize

Tawdry: *from St. Audrey's Fair*

At the Fair of St. Audrey, formerly held in England each year on St. Audrey's Day, October 17, a variety of articles such as laces, gay toys, and the like, were sold. The name *St. Audrey*, shortened to *tawdry*, was used to designate the sort of things one bought at this, or any other, fair: catchpenny articles for the most part, cheap, gaudy, without taste.

Taxicab: *from cabriolet, a carriage that bounced like a goat*

Taxicab is an abbreviation of *taximeter-cabriolet*—a vehicle carrying an instrument for automatically registering the fare. Before the days of the automobile, a *cabriolet* was a light, horse-drawn carriage. The name *cabriolet* is the diminutive of the French *cabriole*, "a leap" like that of a goat, and was applied to this type of carriage because, being light, it bounced on a rough road. French *cabriole* was borrowed from Italian *capriola*, "a somersault," from Latin *caper*, "a he-goat," *capra*, "a she-goat."

Thrill: *originally, to pierce*

Thrill comes to us from the Middle English *thrillen*, "to pierce." The early meaning of *thrill* was

Taxicab

"to perforate with a pointed instrument," "to transfix." This meaning is now obsolete, but from it has developed the modern figurative meaning "to effect emotionally as if by something that pierces," "to penetrate and pervade with delight or horror."

Thug: *from a religious fraternity of India*

A religious fraternity in Northern India practised murder in honor of its god and derived its chief support from plunder. It was suppressed by the British in 1840. A member of this fraternity was called in Hindustani *thag* (pronounced *thug*), "deceiver, robber." English borrowed this as *thug*, to denote "a ruffian," "an assassin."

Torch: *a twisted rag for a wick*

The Latin word *torquere* means "to twist." Because a certain kind of collar was made by twisting, it was called *torqua*, a derivative of *torquere*. This *torqua* became French *torche*, "rag," "torch." English borrowed the word as *torch*.

This Latin word *torquere*, "to twist," has given us a number of other English words. *Torment* is from Old French *torment*, *tourment*, from Latin *tormentum*, meaning "an engine for hurling missiles," operated by turning a crank or windlass, and hence, the word was applied also to a rack, an instrument of torture; *tormentum* is from *torquere*. *Torture* is from Latin *tortura*, another derivative of *torquere*. *Distort*, "to twist out of natural shape," is formed from *dis*, "away," and *torquere*, "to twist." *Extort* is from *torquere* with the prefix *ex*, "out of," giving us the meaning "to wring (money) out of" someone. *Retort*, a recurved, bent-back flask, is from *torquere* with the prefix *re-*, "back." *Contort* is *torquere* combined with *con*, "together."

Torrent and Torrid: *etymological twins*

It seems strange that two words with meanings so different as *torrent* and *torrid* should be derived from the same source. Latin *torrere*, "to burn," "to dry by heat," has a participle *torrens*, "burning," hence "boiling" and "roaring." It was the sense of "boiling" or "roaring" that survived in the borrowed English word *torrent*, a violent stream of water. From the same *torrere* came Latin *torridus* meaning "burning," "parched," the origin of our word *torrid*. Thus we find that the *torrential* rain and the *torrid* sun, although quite opposite in meaning, are closely related etymologically.

Trophy

L. SZANTO

Trivial: *at the crossroads*

Latin *trivium* was a place where "three roads" meet, "the crossroads," formed from *tri-*, "three," and *via*, "way." The adjective *trivialis* means "that may be found at any crossroads," hence, "found anywhere," "common." English borrowed this as *trivial*, originally, "common," "ordinary," and so "of little worth or importance," "trifling."

Trophy: *where the enemy turned and fled*

Greek *tropē* meant "a turn," especially a turning about of the enemy. From this word was formed *tropaion*, "a monument of the enemy's defeat." Latin borrowed this as *tropaeum*, also *trophaeum*; French, in turn, borrowed this as *trophée*; and English borrowed the French form as *trophy*. The word now means, broadly, a thing taken from the enemy and preserved as a memorial of victory.

Ultramarine: *from beyond the sea*

Lapis lazuli was originally brought from "beyond the sea" (Latin *ultra*, "beyond," plus *mare*, "the sea"), that is, from Asia. The adjective *ultramarine*, literally, "oversea," was applied to the blue

Volume

pigment prepared by powdering the imported lapis lazuli. Nowadays *ultramarine* blue may be fairly closely imitated by chemical processes, and quite cheaply.

Vandal: *one of the sackers of Rome*

In the year 455 A.D., a Germanic people, the *Vandals*, who had overrun Gaul, entered Italy and sacked Rome, destroying many monuments of art and literature. Because of their stupid ruthlessness, the name *vandal* has been given to anyone who wantonly mars a beautiful or useful thing.

Volume: *a roll of writing*

In ancient times when papyrus was prepared for writing, the separate pieces were pasted or glued together in one long sheet usually from five to eight inches wide, and then rolled up on a short rod. As the work was written, and later read, it was gradually unrolled from one staff and at the same time rolled up again on another. The Latin word for such a written document was *volumen*, "a roll" of writing, derived from *volvere*, "to roll." This was borrowed in French as *volume*, and this borrowed, in turn, in English. The word has kept pace with improvements in the mate-

Yuletide

rials and form of books, and *volume* now means paper cut in sheets, folded and sewed, and usually with a pair of stiff cover boards to preserve it.

Yuletide: *a jolly time*

Yuletide and the great yule log that was formerly an important part of its ceremony are among our oldest traditions.

The history of the word *yule* is dimmed a little by the mists of time. But we know that its Medieval English form was *yol*, from still older Anglo-Saxon *géol*, and that it is akin to Icelandic *jol*, the midwinter feast (going back to heathen times). This word *jol* may also be the ancestor of *jolly*. So *Yuletide* from the beginning, perhaps, meant "a jolly time," as it still does, although now in its special Christmas significance.

Centaur

A Few Words of Interesting Origin, Classified

Common Flowers *with romantic names*

Many a delightful little story or metaphor is hidden in the names of the flowers. Ancient mythology contributes some of these interesting names. *Dianthus* was sacred to the Greek god Zeus, for its name means, literally, "the flower of Zeus," from *Dios*, "of Zeus," and *anthos*, "flower." *Centaurea* takes its name from Greek *centauros*, meaning "centaur," because Chiron, the centaur, is supposed to have discovered its medicinal properties. The *hyacinth* is named after the youth *Hyacinthus* because it is fabled to have sprung from the blood of this youth when he was slain by Apollo. *Paion*, the Greek god of healing, gave his name to *peony*. The reputed curative values of some flowers account for their names—for example, *sage*, from French *sauge*, which comes from Latin *salvia*, from *salvus*, "saved." Resemblances, real or imagined, to animal shapes account for some of our flower names. *Dandelion* is from French *dent de lion*, "lion's tooth." The nectary or spur of the *delphinium* suggests the shape of the dolphin; so the flower takes its name from Greek *delphis*, "dolphin." The *geranium* bears a fruit suggesting the bill of a crane; so the plant gets its name from

Greek *geranos*, "crane." The naming of *snapdragon* can easily be understood when one examines the blossom and sees its voracious little mouth. It is natural that the sun should affect some of the flower names. *Helianthus* is a "sunflower," from the Greek *hēlios*, "sun," and *anthos*, "flower." *Heliotrope* is one that "turns toward the sun," for its name is a combination of Greek *hēlios*, "sun," and *trepein*, "to turn." Then there is the "windflower"—*anemone*, from Greek *anemos*, "wind"; and the "star flower"—*aster*, from Greek *astēr*, "star." *Chrysanthemum* is, literally, the "golden flower," for its name is from Greek *chrysos*, "gold," and *anthemon*, "flower." Whoever named the *tulip* thought it looked like a turban, for *tulip* comes from the Turkish *tulbend*, "a turban." The first of the month among the ancient Romans was called *kalendae*, "the calends." There was a plant supposed to bloom at that time which was therefore called *calendula*. The bell-shaped blossoms of the *campanula* explain its name which means, in Latin, "little bell." The *carnation*, which has been in cultivation for over two thousand years, was originally flesh-colored; hence its name, which comes from Latin *carnatio*, "fleshiness," from *caro*, genitive *carnis*, "flesh." The *daisy* is from Anglo-Saxon *daeges-éage*, "day's eye." *Digitalis* is named, because of its finger-shaped corolla, from Latin *digitus*, "finger." *Gladiolus* is a Latin word meaning "a small sword," and the name was given to the plant because of its sword-shaped leaves. The leaves of the *hepatica*, on the other hand, suggest the shape of the liver; hence its name, from Latin *hepaticus* (feminine *hepatica*), "of the liver." Anyone who has seen a bed of *iris* in bloom will understand why the Latin word *iris*, "rainbow," was borrowed as the name of this colorful flower. *Narcissus* is named, in allusion to its narcotic properties, from Greek *narkē*, "torpor." "There is pansies, that's for thoughts," said Ophelia, truly enough. *Pansy* comes from French *pensée*, "thought," also the name of this little flower. The red varieties of *phlox* must have been known first, for the name is borrowed from Greek *phlox*, "flame." *Rhododendron* is, literally, "a rose tree," from the Greek *rhodon*, "rose," and *dendron*, "tree." The *nasturtium* is a "nose-twister." Its name comes from Latin *nasus*, "nose," and *torquere*, "to twist," because its pungent taste causes one to make a wry face.

Bird Names *often pithily descriptive*

It is surprising to find how frequently the names of our birds contain, in themselves, pithy little descriptions or interesting side lights on habit or habitat. *Flamingo*, from Spanish or Portuguese, is named for its color, from Latin *flamma*, "flame." The *nightingale* sings in the night, and that is the literal meaning of its name. The word comes straight down from Anglo-Saxon *nihtegale*, from *niht*, "night," and *galan*, "to sing." *Oriole* is a "golden" bird, taking its name from Latin *aureo-*

lus, "golden." *Penguin* is, literally, "a white head," from Welsh *pen,* "head," and *gwyn,* "white." *Plover* means "the rain bird." Its name is taken from Latin *pluere,* "to rain." *Canary* presents a curious case. The name was given to the bird because it was first taken from the Canary Islands. But the Islands are said to have been so named from their large dogs ("dog" in Latin is *canis*). So the *canary* bird has a name which means "dog."

Animal Names *of surprising aptness*

Caterpillar means, literally, "a hairy she-cat," the word being derived from Old (North) French *catte* (French *chatte,* "she-cat") and *pelue,* "hairy." *Chameleon* is a "ground lion," from Greek *chamai,* "on the ground," and *leōn,* "lion." *Dinosaur* means "terrible lizard," coming from Greek *deinos,* "terrible," and *sauros,* "lizard." *Dromedary* was originally a camel of unusual speed, bred for riding, and its (Latin) name was taken from Greek *dromas,* "running." Their habit of honeycombing the earth gave the *gophers* their name, from French *gaufre,* "honeycomb." *Hippopotamus* is a "river horse," Greek *hippopotamos,* from Greek *hippos,* "horse," and *potamos,* "river." The *ichneumon* hunts out the eggs of the crocodile and so is called, literally, "the tracker," from Greek *ichneuein,* "to track or hunt after," from *ichnos,* "track," "footstep." The *lemur,* from its habit of going abroad at night, is called "ghost," Latin *lemur,* a hypothetical singular from *lemures,* "ghosts." The *orang-outang* is a "man of the woods," its name coming from Malay *ōrang,* "man," and *ūtan,* "forest." The grace of the *porpoise* deserves a better name, but its face is responsible. *Porpoise,* literally, "hog-fish," was Middle English *porpeys,* borrowed from Old French, literally, *porc,* "hog," *peis,* "fish," from Latin *porcus,* "swine," and *piscis,* "fish." *Reptile* and *serpent* are both "creeping" things. The former is named from Latin *repere* and the latter from Latin *serpere,* both words meaning "to creep." The *rhinoceros* is named for the horns on his snout, from Greek *rhinos,* "of the nose," and *keras,* "horn." The *spider* is named from the verb *spin.*

Textiles *tracing their own origin*

Calico was first imported from *Calicut* (Madras) in the East Indies and derived its name from its original source. *Crinoline* was a cloth originally woven of horsehair and linen thread, and so its name was made up from Latin *crinis,* meaning "hair." *Damask* takes its name from the city *Damascus,* being formerly "silk of Damascus." *Khaki* is a Hindustani word meaning "dust-colored." Anglo-Saxon *līn,* "flax," gave us the word *linen,* "made of flax." *Mosul,* a city in Mesopotamia, gave its name to *muslin. Nainsook* was highly regarded in India, where it originated, and so was called in Hindustani *nainsukh*, literally, "delight of the eye." *Poplin* was first made at Avignon, a papal town; hence, the material was called in Italian *papalino*, meaning "papal," borrowed in French as *papeline*, *popeline*, and from French into English as *poplin*.

Gems *reflecting fact and fancy*

The ancient Greeks knew a purple stone that they considered to be a talisman against drunkenness; so they called the stone *amethystos*, from *a-*, "not," and *methyein*, "to be drunken," from *methy*, "strong drink." This is our *amethyst*. The *aquamarine* has a beautifully descriptive name, taken from Latin *aqua marina*, "sea water," suggested by its color. *Garnet* is named after the pomegranate (Latin *granatum*) because of its resemblance in shape and color to the seeds of the pomegranate. *Jade* (the name was borrowed from French) was supposed to be effective in curing a pain in the side and therefore was called in Spanish *piedra de ijada*, "stone of the side"; hence, the word *jade*. Latin *rubere*, "to be red," is the origin of *ruby*. *Turquoise* is from French, meaning properly, "Turkish," applied to the stone because it was first brought from Turkey.